UNITED STATES V. CLARK

Second Edition

United States
v.
Clark

Second Edition

Donald Q. Cochran
Associate Professor
Belmont School of Law

National Institute for Trial Advocacy

© 2014 by the National Institute for Trial Advocacy

All rights reserved. No part of this work may be reproduced or transmitted in any form or by any means, electronic or mechanical, including photocopying and recording, or by any information storage or retrieval system without the prior written approval of the National Institute for Trial Advocacy unless such copying is expressly permitted by federal copyright law.

Law students who purchase this NITA publication as part of their class materials and attendees of NITA-sponsored CLE programs are granted a limited license to reproduce, enlarge, and electronically or physically display, in their classrooms or other educational settings, any exhibits or text contained in the printed publication or on the accompanying CD/DVD disk. However, sharing one legally purchased copy of the publication among several members of a class team is prohibited under this license. Each individual is required to purchase his or her own copy of this publication. *See* 17 U.S.C. § 106.

Address inquiries to:
Reprint Permission
National Institute for Trial Advocacy
1685 38th Street, Suite 200
Boulder, CO 80301-2735
Phone: (800) 225-6482
Fax: (720) 890-7069
E-mail: permissions@nita.org

ISBN 978-1-60156-427-6
FBA 1427

17 16 15 14 10 9 8 7 6 5 4 3 2 1
Printed in the United States of America

Official co-publisher of NITA.
WKLegaledu.com/NITA

Contents

Case Summary 1

Indictment 3

Affidavit for Arrest Warrant—Jean Thomas 5

Exhibits in Support of Affidavit for Arrest Warrant 7
    House Diagram 9
    Aerial Photo of Bank—Marked 11
    Aerial Photo of Bank and Location of Car—Marked 13

Witness Statements 15
    Pat Clemons 17
    William Cole 19
    William Cole (Grand Jury Testimony) 21
    Andre Clark 27
    Dolores Dooley 29

Plea Agreement and Conditions—William Cole 31

Memorandum from Special Agent Thomas re Driving Distance Report 35

Memorandum from Special Agent Thomas re Clothing 37

DNA Report—Sean Taylor 39

Expert CV—Sean Taylor 43

Memorandum from Sean Taylor re Information on DNA Evidence 47

Treatise on DNA Evidence 49

Photo Exhibits and Diagrams 53
    Bank Floor Plan 55
    Bank Robbery Photo 09:38:23A 57
    Bank Robbery Photo 09:38:40A 59
    Bank Robbery Photo 09:39:48A 61

Bank Robbery Photo 09:39:51A	63
Bank Robbery Photo 09:39:56A	65
Aerial View of Bank	67
Aerial View of Bank and Location of Chevy Cavalier	69
Chevy Cavalier	71
Maroon Dodge	73
House Diagram	75
Shotgun and Revolver	77
Bag of Money	79
Bathroom	81
Money Found in Bathroom	83
Money Recovered	85
House	87

JURY INSTRUCTIONS **89**

VERDICT FORM **93**

Acknowledgments

The contributions of several people deserve special attention. Angelo Della Manna, Chief of Forensic Biology and DNA at the Alabama Department of Forensic Sciences in Birmingham, Alabama, provided invaluable assistance in helping the author draft the DNA report and accompanying documents.

Tracy Luke, my administrative assistant, greatly assisted me in all aspects of preparing the case file.

Case Summary

On September 23, YR-1, at approximately 9:30 a.m., three individuals entered and robbed the Nita City branch of Main Street Bank located at 825 Main Street, Nita City, Nita, of approximately $18,000. The Government and the Defendant stipulate that the Main Street Bank is a federally insured institution located in the Northern District of Nita.

Investigation at the bank following the robbery determined that three individuals entered the bank yelling to the tellers that a robbery was in progress. One robber vaulted the teller counter area and another brandished a silver revolver. All three were wearing masks and heavy clothing. The third robber, brandishing a sawed-off shotgun, ran into the manager's office while the other two robbers were collecting the money.

The three robbers then fled the bank in a white Chevrolet Cavalier, which was later determined to have been stolen the day before the robbery. The robbers drove several blocks, switched the stolen Cavalier, and entered another car prepositioned at that location.

The Nita City 911 operator received a call from an individual who said he had seen three individuals run from the bank with masks on. The caller told the 911 operator that he was following the car at a distance to see where it went. Several minutes later, the caller stated that he saw the three individuals switch from the white Cavalier to a maroon Dodge sedan. Several minutes after that, the caller told the 911 operator that he saw the maroon Dodge pull behind a house located at 708 Borden Avenue, Nita City, Nita. The individual making the call did not identify himself and has not been identified or located.

Based on the 911 call, Nita Bureau of Investigation (NBI) Special Agent Jean Thomas led a team of NBI agents and Nita City police officers to 708 Borden Avenue. Agent Thomas knocked on the door, and Andre Clark answered the door. Agent Thomas and the other officers and agents surrounded the house and demanded that everyone come outside. William Cole and Jason Fleming came out of the house. William Cole, Andre Clark, and Jason Fleming were all placed face down on the ground and searched. No weapons were found on their persons.

Agent Thomas asked Jason Fleming if he lived at the house, and Fleming responded that he did. Thomas asked for permission to search the residence, and Jason Fleming said he could. Inside the house at 708 Borden Avenue the agents found a stainless steel revolver and a sawed-off shotgun under the cushion of the sofa in the living room. They also found 1) a semiautomatic handgun in a dresser drawer in one of the bedrooms; 2) a blue and white cloth bag; 3) money wrappers; 4) approximately $12,000 in U.S. currency (approximately $6,000 behind the toilet in the bathroom and $6,000 in one of the bedrooms); and 5) in a closet, a homemade hood with two eye-holes cut in it.

All three individuals were indicted for bank robbery in one indictment. William Cole has pled guilty to the one-count indictment, but has not yet been sentenced. He has agreed to testify for the Government. The cases against Andre Clark and Jason Fleming have been severed for trial, and the trial against Andre Clark is proceeding first. Jason Fleming will be tried at a later time.

For use in a full trial the following witnesses are available for the United States:

Pat Clemons

Jean Thomas

William Cole

The following witnesses are available for the Defendant:

Andre Clark

Dolores Dooley

The DNA chemist, Sean Taylor, may be called by either party.

IN THE UNITED STATES DISTRICT COURT

FOR THE NORTHERN DISTRICT OF NITA

UNITED STATES OF AMERICA	)	
	)	
v.	)	CR 00–1234
	)	
JASON FLEMING,	)	
WILLIAM COLE, and	)	
ANDRE CLARK	)	

INDICTMENT

COUNT ONE: 18 U.S.C. §§ 2113(a) & (d) and § 2: Bank Robbery The Grand Jury charges:

On or about the 23rd day of September, YR-1, within the Northern District of Nita, the defendants,

JASON FLEMING,

WILLIAM COLE,

and ANDRE CLARK,

each aided and abetted by the other, unlawfully and by force and violence and by intimidation through the use of dangerous weapons, that is, firearms, did take from the presence of bank tellers approximately $18,032 in United States currency, which said sum of money was in the care, custody, control, management, and possession of Main Street Bank, Nita City, Nita, the deposits of which were then and there insured by the Federal Deposit Insurance Corporation; and the aforesaid defendants, in committing these acts, did assault Pat Clemons and put in jeopardy the life of Pat Clemons by the use of said dangerous weapons in violation of Title 18, United States Code, Sections 2113(a) and (d) and Section 2.

A TRUE BILL

FOREMAN OF THE GRAND JURY

James S. Jones
JAMES S. JONES
United States Attorney

Franklin E. Stanton
FRANKLIN E. STANTON
Assistant United States Attorney

AFFIDAVIT FOR ARREST WARRANT

SUSPECTS: JASON FLEMING, WILLIAM COLE, ANDRE CLARK

Affiant is Jean Thomas, who has been employed by the NBI for over twelve years and is currently assigned to the Nita City Field Division in Nita City, Nita. Affiant has determined the following through observation, interviews, and discussions with other law enforcement personnel.

On September 23, YR-1, at approximately 9:45 a.m., I was in the Nita City, Nita, area preparing to conduct an interview on an unrelated case. I heard a call come over the radio in my car indicating that a bank robbery was in progress at the Nita City branch of Main Street Bank, located at 825 Main Street, Nita City, Nita. I began to head toward that location and had almost reached the bank when a second call came over the radio indicating a 911 caller had said that the persons who committed the robbery were in a maroon Dodge sedan and had gone to a residence located at 708 Borden Avenue, Nita City, Nita. The caller said the Dodge had parked behind the house. I then headed toward the Borden Avenue location, arriving at 708 Borden Avenue at approximately 10:05 a.m.

Upon arriving at 708 Borden Avenue, I parked on the street in front of the house. I did not see any vehicles at the residence. I then walked around to the side of the house and saw that a maroon Dodge sedan, license NTA 998, was parked directly behind the house, close enough to the house that the passenger side doors could not be fully opened. This vehicle was not visible from the front of the house. There was no paved driveway to the back of the house nor was there any indication that vehicles had previously parked behind the house.

When I walked back around to the front of the house, two marked police vehicles from the Nita City Police Department were arriving at the scene. With these two police officers providing backup, I knocked on the door of the residence. An individual identifying himself as Andre Clark answered the door. The backup officers and I placed this individual face down on the ground and searched him. I then had one of the other officers use the speaker in his police car to call out to any others inside the house and demand that everyone come outside. Two individuals who later identified themselves as William Cole and Jason Fleming came out of the house. They were also placed face down on the ground and searched. No weapons were found on any of the three persons.

I asked Jason Fleming if he lived at the house, and Fleming responded that he did. I asked for permission to search the residence, and Jason Fleming gave permission. Inside the house at 708 Borden Avenue I found a stainless steel revolver and a sawed-off shotgun under the cushion of the sofa in the living room. Also found were 1) a semiautomatic handgun in a dresser drawer in one of the bedrooms; 2) a blue and white cloth bag in the bathtub; 3) money wrappers under the sofa in the living room; 4) $12,189 in U.S. currency ($6,147 in a yellow plastic bag behind the toilet in the bathroom, and $6,042 under the mattress in one of the bedrooms); and (5) in a closet, a homemade mask with two eye-holes cut in it (see attached diagram). The mask appeared to be the same type seen in the surveillance photos taken by bank security cameras. After searching the house, I placed Fleming, Cole, and Clark under arrest for bank robbery and had the Nita City officers take them to the Nita City jail.

At this time, I was notified by radio that a white Chevrolet Cavalier matching the description of the car used in the robbery had been located in an alley a short distance from the bank (see aerial photo for location). I went to that location and found a Chevy Cavalier, Nita license plate number NTA 123. Further investigation revealed that the Chevrolet automobile had been reported stolen the previous night.

I returned to the Nita City branch of Main Street Bank and interviewed bank teller Pat Clemons. Other agents interviewed the other tellers and the branch manager. The branch manager informed me that bank records indicated that $18,032 in U.S. currency was missing from the bank.

Through my supervisor, I requested that an evidence collection team be sent to the Nita City branch of Main Street Bank. An NBI Evidence Response Team processed the crime scene at the bank for fingerprint or other evidence. The team also processed the Cavalier, the house at 708 Borden Avenue, and the Dodge automobile found behind the house.

I went to the Nita City jail to interview the three suspects. Suspect Jason Fleming refused to speak with me. Suspects William Cole and Andre Clark spoke voluntarily with me. Based on the interview of suspect Andre Clark, I went to 1814 Avenue Z, Nita City, Nita, the address that Clark had provided for Ms. Dolores Dooley. Ms. Dooley was present at the residence, but indicated that she did not wish to speak with me.

I had medical personnel at the Nita City jail obtain oral swabs from all three suspects. Later that same day (9/23/YR-1), I took these swabs, along with the hood found in the closet at 708 Borden Avenue, to the Nita Department of Forensic Sciences in Nita City, Nita, for examination. The items were given directly to the forensic chemist, who performed the analysis.

Further investigation in the case revealed that suspect Andre Clark was convicted in the Circuit Court of Nita County, Nita, of Theft in the Second Degree for shoplifting. The date of the conviction was September 14, YR-12. Clark was sentenced to two years in prison. Prison records indicate that Clark was released from prison on January 1, YR-10.

Date: September 23, YR-1

Jean Thomas
Jean Thomas, Special Agent Nita Bureau of Investigation

Bonnie Cox
Notary Public

Exhibits in Support of Affidavit for Arrest Warrant

House Diagram

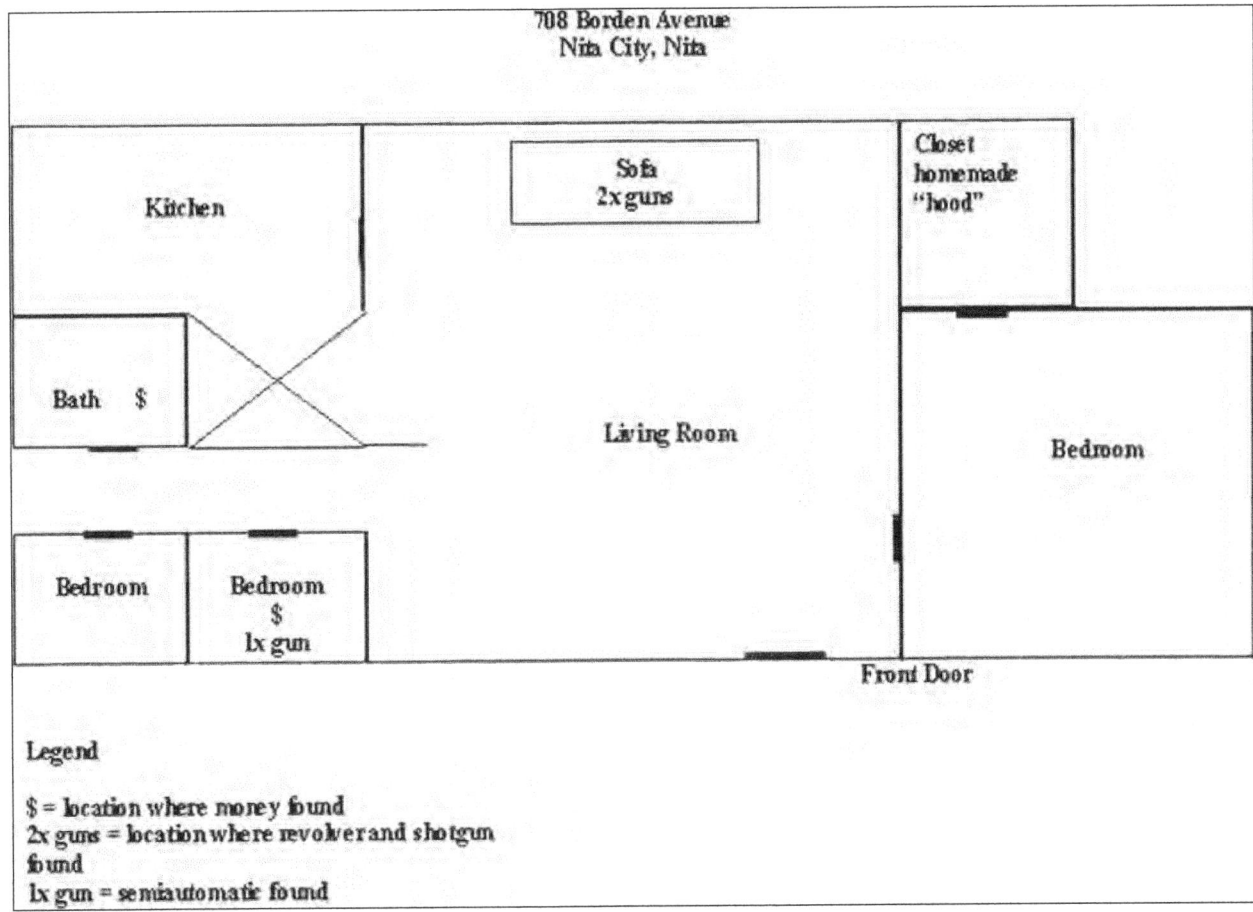

Aerial Photo of Bank – Marked

Aerial Photo of Bank and Location of Car – Marked

Witness Statements

WITNESS STATEMENT OF PAT CLEMONS

Nita Bureau of Investigation   **Date of transcription: 9/29/YR-1**

Pat Clemons was contacted at the Nita City branch of Main Street Bank, 825 Main Street, where she is employed as a teller. Clemons, who was advised of the official identity of the contacting agent by display of credentials, voluntarily provided the following information.

Clemons was sitting at the new accounts desk in the lobby of the bank. Two other tellers (Felicia Jackson and Sandra Fuller) were working behind the teller counter. At approximately 9:30 a.m. Clemons saw an individual with a mask over his head opening the front door to the bank. She noticed immediately that this man was holding a stainless steel handgun and pointing it at her. The man announced: "This is a robbery. Don't touch anything. I'm in a mood to kill someone." The man came to where she was sitting and dragged her out of her chair, pushing her to her knees. The man announced to the other tellers that if they did anything, Clemons would be the first to go. The robber told Clemons "Don't look at me." This individual positioned himself in front of the teller counter and pointed his gun across the counter at the other two tellers and demanded that they come into the bank lobby and sit with their backs against the teller counter. He seemed to be the one in charge.

Another robber entered just after the one with the stainless steel gun and went directly to the manager's office. He had a sawed-off shotgun and hit the manager, Ms. Monroe, with it, screaming at her to get on the floor.

A third robber jumped over the teller counter. This individual was wearing a striped sweater and had a gun stuck in the back of his pants. This robber opened the teller drawers and put the money into a large white bag that he had with him. He was unable to get into Felicia Jackson's teller drawer, as Jackson had locked it and had the key with her in the lobby. The robber with the stainless steel gun grabbed Felicia Jackson by the hair and pulled her to her feet, demanding that she give him the keys. (Ms. Clemons was later shown the bank surveillance photo time stamped 9:39:51A and identified Felicia Jackson as the female in the light-colored clothing.)

About this time, the robber who had gone to the manager's office called out something like, "Let's go—we've been here too long." He ran out of the bank, and the other two followed. Clemons was initially scared, but then got angry at what they had done, so she got up and walked over to the plate glass door and looked out. She saw the three in a small white car, which she thinks was a Chevrolet. The one with the striped sweater was driving as the car sped away. She could not see any of their faces, as they still had masks over their heads.

Case File

Investigation on 9/23/YR-1   at Nita City, Nita

File # YR-1-BH-12345   Date dictated 9/26/YR-1

by SA Jean Thomas

Signed:

Pat Clemons
Pat Clemons

WITNESS STATEMENT OF WILLIAM COLE

Nita Bureau of Investigation   Date of transcription: 9/26/YR-1

William Cole, 5551 Avenue G, Lipscomb, Nita, was interviewed while detained at the Nita City Jail. Cole was advised of the identities of the interviewing agents by display of credentials. Cole was advised of his constitutional right against self-incrimination via the NBI Advice of Rights form. Cole acknowledged he understood his rights, but refused to sign the form. After being advised of the nature of the interview, he provided the following information.

Cole advised he got out of the Nita City Jail thirty days ago, where he was held one year for misdemeanor assault charges and old traffic fines.

Cole advised he went over to Jason Fleming's house at 708 Borden Avenue the night of 9/22/YR-1 and the two went to a club. They went back to Fleming's house, and Cole slept there. Cole did not participate in the robbery because he was sleeping. He said when he got up that morning, only Andre Clark was there. Shortly after he got up, the police arrived.

Investigation on <u>9/23/YR-1</u>   at <u>Nita City, Nita</u>

File # <u>YR-1-BH-12345</u>   Date dictated <u>9/24/YR-1</u>

by <u>SA Jean Thomas</u>

Testimony of

William Cole before the Grand Jury

IMPANELED SEPTEMBER YR-1 AND CONVENED IN

THE NORTHERN DISTRICT OF NITA MEETING IN

ROOM 307

UNITED STATES COURTHOUSE NITA CITY, NITA

Testimony Taken September 29, YR-1

Examination conducted by: FRANKLIN E. STANTON

Assistant United States Attorney Nita City, Nita

SMITH REPORTING SERVICES, INC.

999 NORTH 18th STREET

NITA CITY, NITA 55512

----

1   PROCEEDINGS

3   September 29, YR-1   2:20 p.m.

5   WILLIAM COLE,

7   a witness of lawful age, called before the grand jury and having been first duly sworn, was
8   examined and testified as follows:

10   **EXAMINATION BY MR. STANTON:**

12   Q   Can you tell us your name please?

14   A   William Cole.

16   Q   Do you live in Nita City, Nita?

18   A   Yes.

20   Q   Do you know Jason Fleming?

22   A   Yes.

24   Q   How do you know Jason Fleming?

26   A   We went to high school together and have been friends ever since.

28   Q   Were you involved with Jason Fleming in the robbery of the Nita City branch of Main
29   Street Bank on September 23, YR-1?

31   A   Yes.

33   Q   Tell the grand jury about that.

35   A   Jason had talked about robbing a bank for a long time—maybe several months. He
36   said it would be a good way to get some money. He was out of work. Me, I worked at
37   a temporary job service until I got arrested on this case. Then I got fired. Jason used to
38   work at the funeral home in Nita City. I think that's where he met Andre.

40   Q   Would that be Andre Clark?

42   A   Yes.

1	Q	Did Andre ever talk about robbing a bank?
2		
3	A	I think so. Jason said that Andre said he could get us a car to use for the robbery.
4		
5	Q	Do you know how Andre was going to get the car?
6		
7	A	Jason said he was going to steal it. I know Andre knows how to steal cars. Jason told me
8		he'd done it before.
9		
10	Q	How well did you know Andre?
11		
12	A	Not very well. I just knew Jason, and Jason knew Andre.
13		
14	Q	What happened on September 23?
15		
16	A	I went over to Jason's house that morning.
17		
18	Q	Would that be at 708 Borden Avenue?
19		
20	A	Yes, that's the address.
21		
22	Q	What time did you go over?
23		
24	A	About eight o'clock in the morning.
25		
26	Q	Who was there when you got there?
27		
28	A	Jason and Andre.
29		
30	Q	What happened?
31		
32	A	Jason started saying that we were going to rob the Main Street Bank that morning.
33		
34	Q	Did you know anything about the plan to rob the bank before that morning?
35		
36	A	No. Jason had talked about robbing a bank, but he had never said when.
37		
38	Q	Was there anything unusual at the house?
39		
40	A	There was a white Chevy outside.
41		
42	Q	Had you ever seen that car before?
43		
44	A	No.

1	Q	Where did it come from?
3	A	I assumed that Jason and Andre had stolen it for the robbery.
5	Q	What happened next?
7	A	Jason handed me a sawed-off shotgun and a mask. He said I was going to handle the manager.
10	Q	Did you ask him what he meant by that?
12	A	No, I pretty much knew what to do.
14	Q	What happened next?
16	A	We sat around for a while until we knew the bank was open—Jason said it opened at 9:00. Then we drove over to the bank to check it out. Jason drove the white Chevy, and Andre drove his car—an ugly purple Dodge. I rode with Jason. We parked Andre's car in an alley a couple of blocks from the bank and all got into the Chevy. Andre drove me and Jason over near the bank and parked. Then me and Jason got out and walked around the bank looking for any cops or security. We went back to the Chevy, and all of us put our masks on.
24	Q	Do you remember what everyone was wearing?
26	A	No. Just that it was dark and long sleeved to cover us up. And we all had masks.
28	Q	What happened next?
30	A	Andre drove the Chevy to the bank. We pulled up real fast right in front, in the closest parking space to the front door. Jason jumped out of the front passenger door and ran in first. Andre was the second one in. By the time I went in, Jason was already screaming at a lady in the lobby and Andre was already jumping over the counter to get the money.
36	Q	Was everyone armed?
38	A	I had the sawed-off shotgun Jason gave me. Jason had a stainless steel .357. I know Andre had a pistol with him in the car. I'm pretty sure he took it into the bank.
41	Q	What did you do?
43	A	I went in last and went to the manager's office like Jason told me to. I didn't point the gun at anyone and didn't do anything to hurt anyone. I just wanted to get out of there. Jason just kept yelling that he wanted to kill someone, and I got scared. It seemed like it

was taking forever. I finally yelled out "I'm leaving," and I ran out the door and jumped in the back seat of the car. Jason came out next and jumped in the front passenger seat. Andre was last, and he got in the driver's seat. He backed up real fast, and we drove around the bank, past the drive-through window, and the back of the bank. We took a right on the main road, then another right, then a left into the alley. Andre stopped the Chevy right behind the Dodge we had left in the alley, and we all got out and jumped into the Dodge and Andre took off.

Q   Was anyone wearing latex gloves?

A   I didn't have any gloves on, and I don't think Jason did. I'm not sure about Andre.

Q   What happened to your mask?

A   I threw it out of the car window as we drove to Jason's house.

Q   What happened next?

A   We drove back to Jason's house. When we got there, Jason told Andre to pull around to the back of the house. Andre pulled so close to the house that Jason and I had to get out on the other side of the car. We went right inside and sat down on the living room floor together, and Jason started to divide up the money. He dumped the bag out on the floor and started to toss packets of bills in front of each of the three of us, kind of like dealing cards. When the money was all divided into three piles, we each took ours. Jason put his into some kind of yellow bag and took it back into the back of the house. After a while, maybe fifteen minutes or so, Andre got up and looked out the front window through the curtain. He said, "There's cops out there," and we all scrambled to put stuff away. I grabbed my money and ran back into one of the bedrooms and stuffed it under one of the mattresses. When I came back into the living room, the guns were all gone off the floor. I didn't see what Andre did with his money. Then we heard the loudspeaker say to come outside with our hands up. I went out, and the cops arrested me.

Q   Do any of you ladies and gentlemen in the grand jury have any questions for Mr. Cole?

(No response)

(Whereupon the witness exited the grand jury room at approximately 2:38 p.m.)

END OF PROCEEDINGS

STATEMENT OF ANDRE CLARK

Nita Bureau of Investigation   Date of transcription: 9/28/YR-1

Andre Clark, 423 Morgan Road, Nita City, Nita, was interviewed while detained at the Nita City Jail. Clark was advised of the identities of the interviewing agents by display of credentials. Clark was advised of his constitutional right against self-incrimination via the NBI Advice of Rights form. Clark acknowledged he understood his rights and that he was willing to make a statement. After being advised of the nature of the interview, he provided the following information.

Clark lives by himself at 423 Morgan Road, Nita City, Nita. He said that he works at the Nita City Funeral Home doing odd jobs for the owner and has worked there for approximately three years.

Clark stated that this morning he got up and went by the house of his old girlfriend, Dolores Dooley, who lives at 1814 Avenue Z, Nita City, Nita. He said he went by the house to pick up a set of keys that he had given to Ms. Dooley when they were dating. He stated that he did not have his watch on, but said that he left his house at approximately 9:00 and it takes about fifteen minutes to get to Ms. Dooley's house. He said that he was not there for long—maybe five or ten minutes.

Clark stated that he next went to Jason Fleming's house at 708 Borden Avenue. He met Fleming several years ago when Fleming also worked for the funeral home. He had become friends with Fleming and often visited him at this home. When he arrived at Fleming's house, he parked his car, a maroon 1992 Dodge Dynasty four door, license number NTA 998, behind the residence, as he usually does and then proceeded around to the front of the house. He entered the residence, and inside were Jason Fleming and William Cole sitting in the living room. Clark stated that he doesn't recall what time he arrived at the house, but after he had been there approximately five minutes Cole got up and looked out the window and stated that he saw two police cars in front of the house.

Clark stated that he heard a knock on the door and when he answered the door, an NBI agent told him to lay face down on the ground. He was then searched and arrested.

Clark stated that he did not participate in the bank robbery of the Main Street Bank in Nita City, Nita. He advised that he did not go into the bank, nor was he involved in the bank robbery in any way, nor did he know anything about the bank robbery until the agent told him was under arrest for bank robbery. He advised that prior to the police arriving at the house there was no talk inside the house about any robbery. He also advised that he saw no money or guns inside the house prior to the police arriving.

CASE FILE

Investigation on 9/23/YR-1   at Nita City, Nita

File # YR-1-BH-12345   Date dictated 9/25/YR-1

by SA Jean Thomas

Signed:

Andre Clark
Andre Clark

STATEMENT OF DOLORES DOOLEY

Nita Bureau of Investigation   Date of transcription: 12/29/YR-1

DOLORES DOOLEY, 1814 Avenue Z, Nita City, Nita, was interviewed on December 28, YR-1, at her residence by Special Agent (SA) Jean Thomas and Nita City Police Officer Frank Clemons, who knows Ms. Dooley because the two attended high school together. Dooley was advised of the identity of the interviewing agent and officer. She replied that she was expecting us and she knew why we were there. Writer confirmed it was in reference to Andre Clark and the September 23, YR-1, Main Street Bank robbery. She thereafter provided the following information.

She distinctly remembers September 23, YR-1, the day Andre Clark was arrested for bank robbery. She had a 10:00 a.m. appointment at Dollar Discount, Nita City, Nita, for a job interview that day. She and her neighbor Vanessa Wilson left her apartment between 9:15 and 9:30 a.m. and drove straight to the Dollar Discount. It is approximately a twenty to thirty drive from her house to Dollar Discount, and she was not late for her appointment.

Dooley advised that for several years she and Andre Clark were boyfriend and girlfriend. She broke up with him in August YR-1, approximately one month before the bank robbery, and has only seen him once since then. That singular event occurred around 9:15 a.m. on September 23, YR-1, as Dooley was preparing to leave her apartment for the job interview. Andre Clark knocked on her door and told her he wanted his keys. She thought this was unusual as she had his keys for approximately one month. The keys were described as being twenty or more keys, consisting of house keys, car keys, etc. They did not speak, she advised, as they were mad at each other. Clark was there not more than five minutes. He stayed at the door and did not go into the apartment. Dooley did not notice his car or associates, if any. Dooley further advised she has not talked to him since that day. Dooley advised that none of her children were fathered by Andre Clark.

Dooley stated that it takes approximately fifteen minutes to drive from her house to 708 Borden Avenue and approximately twenty minutes to get from her house to the Nita City branch of Main Street Bank.

Note: It should be noted that while the interview was underway, Andre Clark called Dooley's residence. Dooley explained that Clark calls occasionally to talk to the kids and that she doesn't talk to him. However, it was noted she was on the telephone with him for several minutes (in the kitchen area) and the kids did not spend any time talking to Clark.

CASE FILE

Investigation on 12/28/YR-1   at Nita City, Nita

File # YR-1-BH-12345   Date dictated 12/29/YR-1

by SA Jean Thomas

Signed:

Dolores Dooley
Dolores Dooley

IN THE UNITED STATES DISTRICT COURT FOR

THE NORTHERN DISTRICT OF NITA

UNITED STATES OF AMERICA	)	
	)	
v.	)	CR 00–1234
	)	
WILLIAM COLE	)	

PLEA AGREEMENT AND CONDITIONS

The United States of America and the Defendant hereby acknowledge the following to be the plea agreement between the Defendant and the United States and the conditions and understandings that apply to the agreement:

I. PLEA AGREEMENT: The United States and the Defendant hereby AGREE to the following:

   a. Plea: The Defendant will plead guilty to Count One of the indictment in the above-styled case charging a violation of Title 18, United States Code, Sections 2113(a) and (d) and Section 2, Bank Robbery.

   b. Recommendation: Pursuant to Rule 11(e)(1)(B) of the Federal Rules of Criminal Procedure and upon the Court's acceptance of the aforesaid plea and entry of judgment on the same, the United States will recommend that:

      i. the Defendant receive a sentence at the low end of the guideline range as determined by the Court;

      ii. the Defendant receive credit for acceptance of responsibility;

      iii. if the Defendant provides substantial assistance as defined by the Sentencing Guidelines, the United States will move for a downward departure. The Defendant is aware that the Court will not be bound by this recommendation.

II. CONDITIONS AND UNDERSTANDINGS: The following conditions and understandings apply to the above-stated plea agreement:

POSSIBLE SENTENCES AND THE GUIDELINES

   a. Maximum Possible Sentence: The Defendant is aware that the maximum possible punishment under the statute is twenty-five years. The Defendant is aware that a sentence could include imprisonment, supervised release terms following imprisonment, fines, assessments, restitution, and other costs and losses.

b. Guidelines: Congress has created Sentencing Guidelines which set a sentencing range in this case.

c. The Defendant and the Defendant's attorney are aware of the Sentencing Guidelines and have studied their application to this case. The Defendant is aware that the Court ultimately calculates the guideline sentence range applicable to this case and is not bound by the Defendant's, the Probation Officer's, or the United States Attorney's calculations. Also the Court may impose a sentence above or below the guideline range, up to the maximum possible sentence under the law.

d. Non-binding: It is the Court's duty to impose sentence. The Court is not a party to the above plea agreement. Any sentence recommendation by the United States does not bind the Court, and the Court may impose a more severe or less severe sentence than that recommended.

WITHDRAWAL OF GUILTY PLEA NOT ALLOWED

If the Court decides not to give the recommended sentence, decides that the recommended sentence is not within the Guideline range, or decides to depart from the Guideline range, the Defendant may not withdraw the plea of guilty.

COOPERATION

Should the Defendant provide substantial assistance, the United States will evaluate the assistance and, if justified, make a motion under § 5K1.1 of the Guidelines to lower the sentencing range. The Defendant agrees to cooperate by providing truthful information at all times. The Court is not bound to grant the motion for downward departure. The Court may impose a sentence above or below the guidelines range, even the maximum possible sentence under the law.

ACKNOWLEDGMENTS

1. I have READ this document, DISCUSSED it with my attorney, and UNDERSTAND and AGREE with all its provisions both individually and totally.

September 28, YR-1	*William Cole*
DATE	WILLIAM COLE, Defendant

2. I have reviewed this document and agree to its provisions.

September 28, YR-1	*James S. Jones*
DATE	JAMES S. JONES, United States Attorney

September 28, YR-1	*Franklin E. Stanton*
DATE	FRANKLIN E. STANTON, Assistant United States Attorney

Memorandum

To: Assistant United States Attorney

From: Special Agent Jean Thomas

Ref: Driving distances and times

Date: December 29, YR-1

The following investigation was conducted by Special Agent (SA) JEAN THOMAS on December 28, YR-1, at Nita City, Nita.

Writer measured the distance using a Bureau automobile odometer and timed the driving route between the Main Street Bank and the switch location and 708 Borden Avenue, Nita City, Nita. The results are set forth below:

Bank to switch location

    Distance: 0.2 miles

    Time: 1 minute 20 seconds

Switch location to 708 Borden Avenue

    Distance: 3.4 miles

    Time: 7 minutes 57 seconds

Total (bank to Borden Avenue)

    Distance: 3.6 miles

    Time: 9 minutes 17 seconds

Note: This computation does not account for time spent at the switch location or a different/longer route to 708 Borden Avenue.

Memorandum

To: Assistant United States Attorney

From: Special Agent Jean Thomas

Ref: Defendant Andre Clark clothing

Date: [Monday of the week prior to trial]

You asked me last week to get all the physical evidence ready for trial next week, specifically including the clothing that Andre Clark had on when he was arrested. When he was arrested at 708 Borden Avenue on September 23, YR-1, Andre Clark had on a sweater and baggy pants. The sweater had a pattern that was consistent with the one seen in the surveillance photos from the bank. The clothing was taken from Clark when he was processed at the Nita City Jail. I recall asking the person processing Clark to make sure and save the clothing in their property room. I don't recall that person's name.

Apparently when Clark was released on bail the following week the clothing was given back to him when he left the jail. At any rate, the Nita City police department no longer has either the sweater or the pants.

Additionally, I checked with the NBI crime lab regarding the status of fingerprint evidence in the case. I was informed that none of the fingerprints that were submitted from the bank, the house at 708 Borden Avenue, the maroon Dodge, or the Chevrolet Cavalier had sufficient detail to make an identification. Based on my training and experience, however, it is not unusual for fingerprints taken at a crime scene and submitted for comparison to lack the degree of detail necessary to make a positive identification.

NITA DEPARTMENT OF FORENSIC SCIENCES
DNA REPORT

January 7, YR-0

Re: Case 03BH-12345

Main Street Bank, subject

Andre Clark, suspect

William Cole, suspect

Jason Fleming, suspect

MEMORANDUM: TO FILE

BY: Sean Taylor, Forensic Scientist

SUBJECT: Examination of Biological Evidence

On September 23, YR-1, Special Agent Jean Thomas of the Nita Bureau of Investigation (NBI) submitted to the laboratory certain items of evidence relative to the above-styled case. The following is a description of the evidence and the results of laboratory examinations and analyses:

1. One (1) sealed brown paper bag labeled, in part, ". . . where $ found . . . behind toilet . . . 708 Borden Avenue . . ." containing one (1) tied closed yellow "Dollar Discount" plastic bag. Bag is received torn open in an area adjacent to the tied closed portion of the plastic bag.

2. One (1) sealed brown paper bag labeled, in part, ". . . closet . . . 708 Borden Avenue . . ." containing one (1) brown makeshift cloth mask. Mask is constructed from one (1) uniform section of fabric, stitched along the outer seams, and knotted in the rear. Two (2) makeshift defects acting as eye holes are present along the front of the mask.

3. One (1) sealed brown paper bag labeled, in part, ". . . from bathtub . . . 708 Borden Ave . . ." containing one (1) blue and white canvas tote bag.

4. One (1) sealed manila envelope labeled, in part, ". . . Jason Fleming . . ." containing the following:

    a. One (1) sealed manila envelope containing oral swabs.

    b. One (1) sealed manila envelope identified to contain combed hair samples.

    c. One (1) sealed white envelope identified to contain plucked hair samples.

Page 2
03BH-12345
Examination of Biological Evidence

1. One (1) sealed manila envelope labeled, in part, ". . . William Cole . . ." containing the following:

    a. One (1) sealed manila envelope containing oral swabs.

    b. One (1) sealed manila envelope identified to contain combed hair samples.

    c. One (1) sealed white envelope identified to contain plucked hair samples.

2. One (1) sealed manila envelope labeled, in part, " . . . Andre Clark . . ." containing the following:

    a. One (1) sealed manila envelope containing oral swabs.

    b. One (1) sealed manila envelope identified to contain combed hair samples.

    c. One (1) sealed white envelope identified to contain plucked hair samples.

3. One (1) sealed brown paper bag identified to contain control sample of Puritan cotton-tipped applicators.

RESULTS

The interior surface of the mask (Item 2) exhibited a positive result when tested for components of saliva.

The following items were examined and analyzed for the presence of biological stains, however none were detected:

- plastic bag (Item 1)

- tote bag (Item 3)

The following items were processed for the recovery of trace evidence, with the recovered hair and fiber preserved for further testing:

- plastic bag (Item 1)

- tote bag (Item 3)

Page 3
03BH-12345
Examination of Biological Evidence

The following items were profiled utilizing the D8S1179, D21S11, D7S820, CSF1PO, D3S1358, TH01, D13S317, D16S539, D2S1338, D19S433, vWA, TPOX, D18S51, Amelogenin, D5S818, and FGA DNA typing systems:

- saliva stain, mask (Item 2)
- oral swabs, Jason Fleming (Item 4A)
- oral swabs, William Cole (Item 5A)
- oral swabs, Andre Clark (Item 6A)

REMARKS

The results of DNA typing indicate the following:

- Jason Fleming, William Cole, and Andre Clark are all excluded as potential donors to the saliva recovered from the mask (Item 2).

Sean Taylor
Sean Taylor

SEAN TAYLOR

1234 SMITH STREET • OFFICE: (555) 345–5678

NITA CITY, NITA • FAX: (555) 345–5679

STRENGTHS:

- Court Qualified Forensic Scientist (Biology): State and Federal Court
- Certified by the American Board of Criminalistics
- DNA Databanking Experience:
- NBI CODIS Program, Local and State Levels

EDUCATION:

The University of Nita (UN), Nita City, Nita

- Master of Science in Forensic Science (MSFS), June YR-11
- Selected Outstanding Graduate Student in Forensic Science by Faculty of UN Graduate School, YR-11 Honors Convocation
- Recipient of University Dean's Award, spring YR-11
- Graduate Coursework included:
    - Biological Methods in Forensic Science
    - Advanced Biological Methods in Forensic Science
    - Elements of Forensic Science
    - Law and Evidence
    - Biochemistry
    - Analysis of Trace Evidence

The University of Toronto, Toronto, Ontario, Canada

- Bachelor of Science (BS) Chemistry, June YR-13

PROFESSIONAL SCHOOLS/COURSES ATTENDED:

- Bloodstain Pattern Analysis Workshop
- Metro-Dade Police Department Training Bureau, Miami, FL, YR-8
- DNA Databanks and Repositories Course
- Armed Forces Institute of Pathology, YR-9–YR-8
- Quality Assurance in Forensic DNA Technology Workshop Nita Bureau of Investigation, YR-9
- PCR Based DNA Typing Methods Course Nita Bureau of Investigation, YR-10

FORENSIC SCIENTIST EXPERIENCE:

Employment History

Nita Department of Forensic Sciences - Nita City Laboratory YR-11–present

- Laborer - Biology Section YR-11–YR-9
- Forensic Scientist I - Biology Section YR-9–YR-7
- Forensic Scientist II/III - Biology Section YR-6–YR-2
- Forensic Scientist IV - Biology Section YR-2–present
- Discipline Chief of Forensic Biology YR-2–present

    - Daily duties include directing the Forensic Biology efforts in the regional DNA Laboratories, as well as the statewide DNA Database Laboratory. Overseeing the statewide DNA program involves the development of standard operating protocols, insuring a Laboratory's compliance with FBI National Standards in order to maintain accreditation, and the budgeting and management of State and Federal funds allocated for DNA analysis in criminal casework.

    - Additional duties include the examination of criminal case evidence for the presence of biological stains. These stains are then subjected to PCR based DNA typing with the resulting DNA Profiles compared against known subject and suspect profiles. A report of the findings is written and defended as an expert witness in a court of law.

    - Routinely respond to crime scenes and process the scene for items of physical evidence specifically relating to Biological stains and Trace Evidence.

- Featured on The Discovery Channel Documentary Series "The New Detectives: Case Studies in Forensic Science" episode titled "Double Helix."

- Selected Employee of the Year, Nita Department of Forensic Sciences YR-7.

- Recipient of Significant Contribution to the Forensic Sciences Award, Southern Association of Forensic Sciences YR-7.

- Published Forensic DNA Research findings in the *Journal of Forensic Sciences*.

PROFESSIONAL AFFILIATIONS

- American Academy of Forensic Sciences (AAFS), YR-13–present

- Canadian Society of Forensic Science (CSFS), YR-11–present

Memorandum

To: Assistant United States Attorney

From: Sean Taylor, Forensic Scientist

Ref: Your Request for Information on DNA Evidence

In response to your request several weeks ago for general information on the use of DNA evidence in criminal cases, I have attached a copy of a short treatise that I wrote several months ago. The treatise was prepared for a presentation to the Nita Prosecutors' Association. It should provide you with answers to the general questions you were asking.

TREATISE ON DNA EVIDENCE IN CRIMINAL CASES

DNA stands for deoxyribonucleic acid. It is the basic building block of life, a chemical code that is present in each and every one of us and that has a unique configuration for every individual (with the exception of identical twins). An individual's DNA is present in virtually every cell of their body, and that configuration is the same whether it originates from that person's blood, semen, saliva, or other body tissues. A large portion of the DNA that we all have is the same, as every human being requires certain things to function and live—a heart, brain, lung capacity, etc., and so the areas of the DNA that code for these specific functions are the same within each of us. However, there are other areas or "addresses" on the DNA that are very different within each of us, and that is where the forensic DNA testing community focuses its efforts—on these addresses that have been shown to vary greatly between individuals—thus allowing the testing process to easily delineate between individuals in criminal cases. Using DNA testing in this context, it is possible for the scientist to compare DNA that has been recovered from a bloodstain or other body fluid or body tissue at a crime scene with the DNA of a known individual—a suspect or victim, for example—and determine not only who the donor of the crime scene sample was, but also who may be excluded, all with virtual certainty.

The DNA testing process is divided into three basic steps: 1) extraction, 2) amplification, and 3) visualization.

Once the forensic scientist identifies a possible biological stain on an evidence item, the laboratory testing proceeds from the very general to the very specific. For example, when a stain is first seen on a piece of clothing, the most general question is whether it is a bloodstain at all, or whether it is ketchup, paint, or any number of other substances. The scientist can perform some rapid chemical tests which indicate that the particular stain is indeed a bloodstain. Then, getting more specific, the analyst will determine whether it is human blood or the blood of a deer, dog, cat, etc.

If the follow-up testing proves that the stain is human in origin, then the DNA testing process begins in force, starting with extraction. In this step, the scientist's purpose is to remove the stain from the surface or substrate it is on and obtain the DNA in a liquid form. For example, if a saliva stain has been identified on a cloth, the extraction step would be focused on removing the saliva cells from the cotton substrate and adding specific chemicals that allow the analyst to then have purified DNA in a liquid form, ready for further testing.

Once the extraction step is completed, the scientist will determine how much DNA was recovered from the extraction process and use that information to proceed to the amplification step. In amplification, the scientist uses a process called polymerase chain reaction (PCR) to mimic what our body does every day and make multiple copies of DNA, albeit in a laboratory setting. For example, if you sustain an injury to your hand, hours later a scab may begin to develop. Then, days later, a scar of new skin may be present. Throughout this entire time the body is generating its new skin by making multiple copies of your DNA to regenerate what was injured. In the DNA laboratory, the forensic scientist is employing the same technique and using chemicals that are specifically designed to target those DNA addresses mentioned earlier—those that we know are very different from one individual to another. Once these addresses are found, the scientist makes multiple genetic copies of these specific areas so they are easily visualized in the final step. The extraction step is often compared to acting as a molecular Xerox machine, where billions of DNA copies can be made for easy visualization.

An important note for the amplification step is that the greater the number of "addresses" on the DNA that are tested, the more specific the entire process becomes. Each of the addresses that are examined are independent of one another and thus are informative in and of themselves. The more areas a scientist looks at, the more descriptive the information becomes about who may or may not be the contributor of the crime scene stain.

In the final step, called visualization, the forensic scientist obtains the DNA profile of the crime scene stain, visualized by a series of peaks representing the size of DNA at each location tested, and then compares each and every peak to the reference DNA profile from the suspect(s) or victim(s) in the case to determine who is the source of the crime scene stain. In describing this comparison, I often use the following analogy: if one was to try and describe a vehicle in a parking lot, one trait may be that it is a blue car and another may be that it has tan interior. Clearly these are areas or traits that are independent of one another, as not all cars are blue and not all blue cars have tan interior. Describing a vehicle in this way is comparable to testing for two addresses on the DNA. However, the DNA testing process in a forensic setting now routinely analyzes crime scene samples in up to sixteen different areas, generating a very clear profile of traits that may be compared to a suspect. This is comparable to being able to describe the vehicle in our analogy as a blue car, tan interior, 2009 model, tinted windows, four door, scratch on the front bumper, and on and on for up to sixteen traits that are all independent of each other.

Finally, at the end of the testing process, the forensic scientist compares the DNA profile from the crime scene sample to the reference samples and determines if any match or do not match. It is important to note that the true power of DNA is in its ability to *exclude* falsely accused individuals. If any one of the up to sixteen different addresses does not match, then the individual is *absolutely excluded* as the source of the crime scene stain. By contrast, if the DNA profile matches at each and every one of the addresses, then the scientist and the trier of fact need to know how significant the match is. That is, is the DNA profile present in the crime scene stain one that is extremely common in the population or is it extremely rare? To answer this question, the forensic scientist employs population genetics. Population genetics allow the scientist to ascertain how often the particular DNA profile may be expected to occur in a reference population of Caucasians and African-Americans. Because each of the sixteen addresses is independent of one another, the frequency associated with each location on the DNA is multiplied together. Using this method, it is not uncommon to generate extremely rare population frequencies, often rarer than the "one in 280 billion" threshold that allows the scientist to offer an opinion that the profile did originate from that specific individual (or his or her identical twin) to the exclusion of all others. (This threshold was chosen because it currently represents about 1,000 times the population of the United States.)

Also it is important to mention the fact that the DNA testing processes employed in the forensic setting and described above are not novel methods, but have been generally accepted in the scientific community as reliable for decades and withstood numerous reviews associated with their validation, reproducibility, and reliability. When DNA testing first began to emerge in the forensic community in the late 1980s, the National Research Council (National Academy of Sciences) studied the genetic basis for the testing, determined its reliability, and published two reports, one in 1992 and one in 1996, both of which affirmed the validity and reliability of forensic DNA testing. In addition, an extensive study by the Office of Technology Assessment (the analytical arm of the U.S. Congress) was published in 1990, also declaring forensic DNA tests both valid and reliable.

Finally, it is important to also understand the limitations of DNA technology. While the advantages of this testing are numerous and well documented, it is important to recognize that the current processes employed in DNA testing are not capable of "dating" a biological stain and thus cannot determine *when* a crime scene stain was deposited. Similarly, it should also be recognized that individuals may travel through crime scenes or wear articles of clothing and not leave traces of their DNA behind. Thus, the absence of DNA at a crime scene does not necessarily equate to the absence of the individual from the area.

Sean Taylor
Sean Taylor Forensic Scientist

Photo Exhibits and Diagrams

Bank Floor Plan

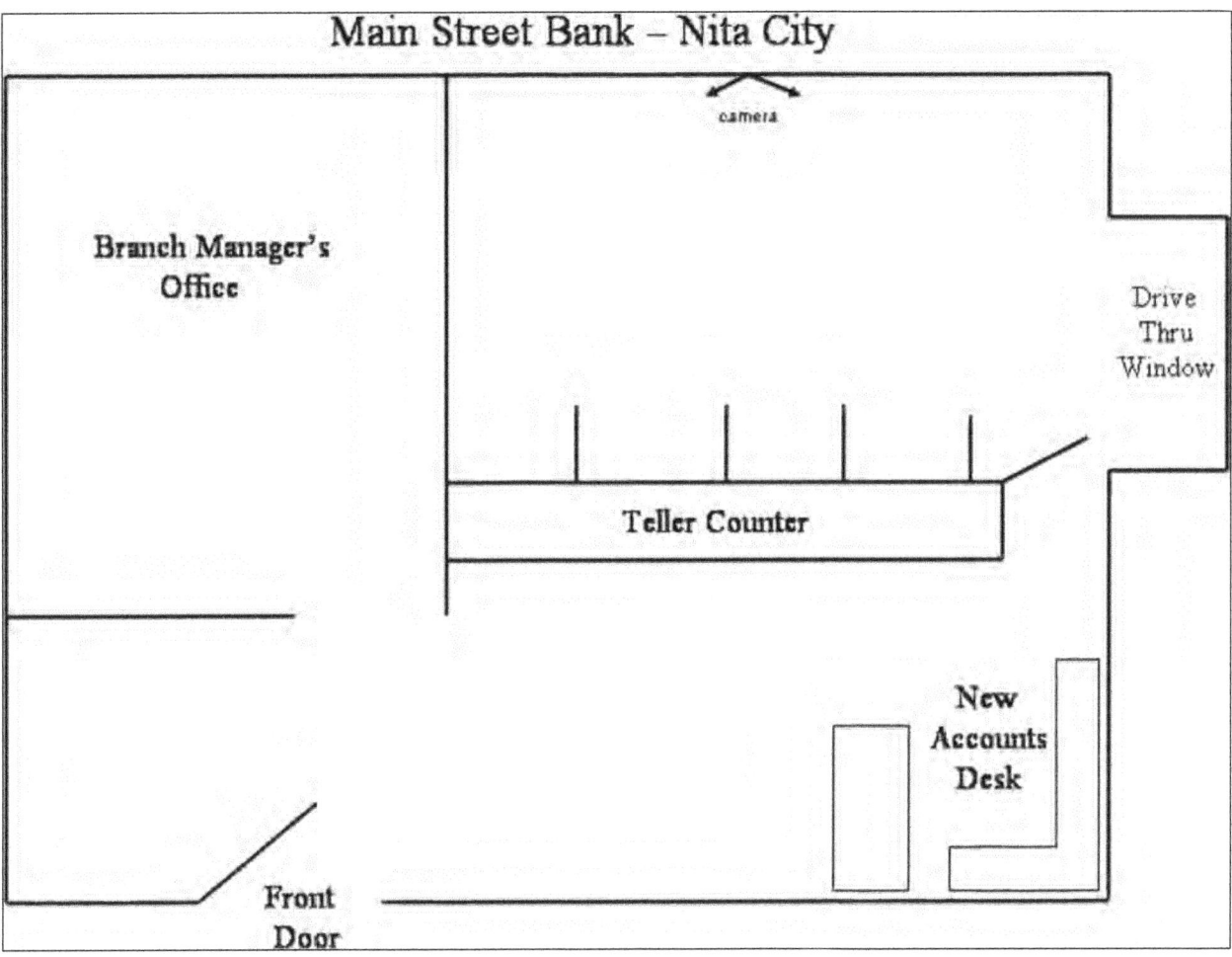

Bank Robbery Photo 09:38:23A

Bank Robbery Photo 09:38:40A

Bank Robbery Photo 09:39:48A

Bank Robbery Photo 09:39:51A

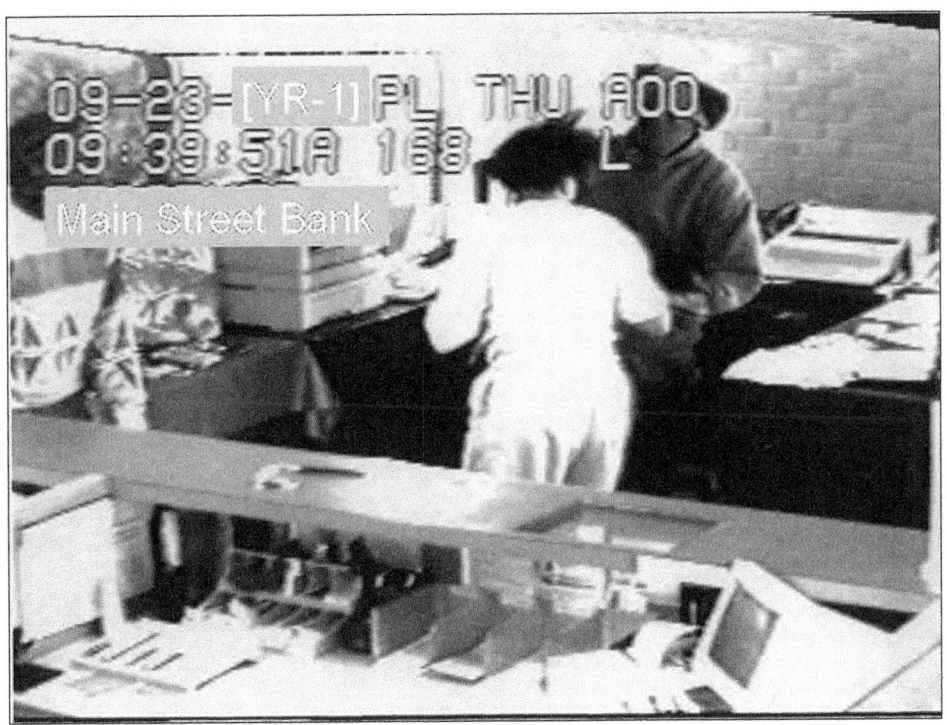

Bank Robbery Photo 09:39:56A

Aerial View of Bank

Aerial View of Bank and Location of Chevy Cavalier

Chevy Cavalier

Maroon Dodge

House Diagram

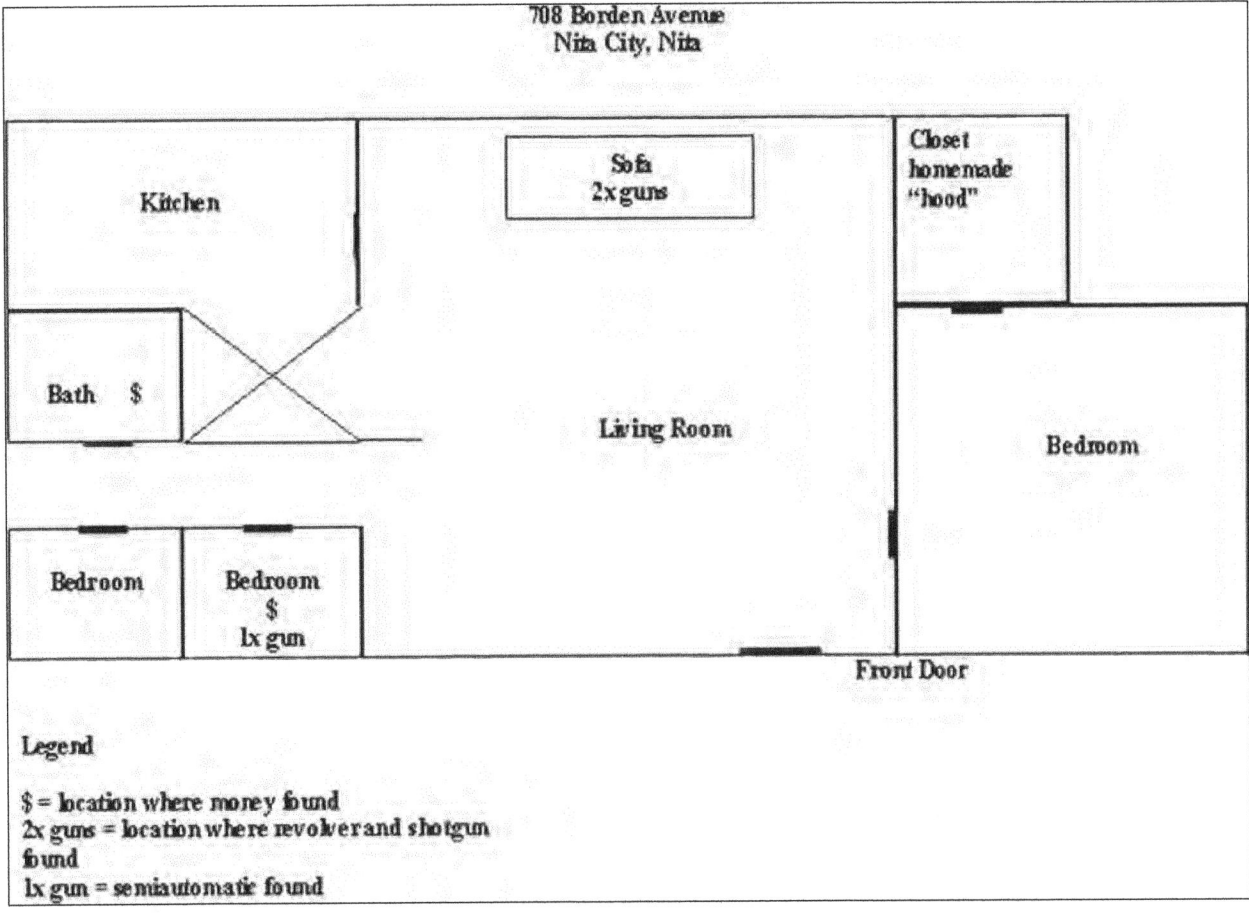

Shotgun and Revolver

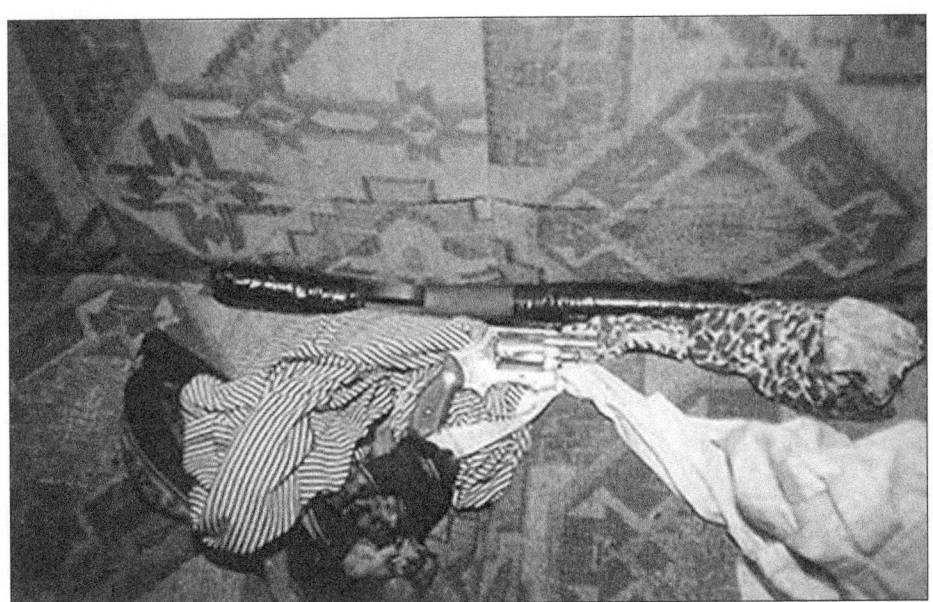

Bag of Money

Bathroom

Money Found in Bathroom

Money Recovered

House 708 Borden Avenue

Jury Instructions

You have now heard all of the evidence in the case.

It is now my duty to instruct you on the rules of law that you must follow and apply in arriving at your decision in this case.

In any jury trial there are, in effect, two judges.

I am one of the judges. It is my duty to preside over the trial and to determine what testimony and evidence is relevant under the law for your consideration.

It is also my duty at the end of the trial to instruct you on the law applicable to the case. You jurors are the other judge—you judge the facts.

But in determining what actually happened in this case—that is, in reaching your decision about the facts—it is your sworn duty to follow the law I am now in the process of defining for you.

The indictment or formal charge against a defendant is not evidence of guilt. Indeed, the defendant is presumed by the law to be innocent.

The law does not require a defendant to prove his or her innocence or to produce any evidence at all.

The Government has the burden of proving a defendant guilty beyond a reasonable doubt, and if it fails to do so, you must acquit the defendant.

While the Government's burden of proof is a strict or heavy burden, it is not necessary that the defendants' guilt be proved beyond all possible doubt.

It is only required that the Government's proof exclude any reasonable doubt concerning the defendants' guilt.

A "reasonable doubt" is a real doubt; it is a doubt based on reason and common sense, after careful and impartial consideration of all the evidence in the case.

Proof beyond a reasonable doubt, therefore, is proof of such a convincing character that you would be willing to rely and act on it, without hesitation, in the most important of your own affairs.

If you are convinced that the accused has been proved guilty beyond a reasonable doubt, say so. If you are not convinced, say so.

If the Government calls William Cole as a witness

Testimony of some witnesses must be considered with more caution than the testimony of other witnesses.

In this case, the Government called as one of its witnesses a person with whom the Government has entered into a plea agreement providing for the possibility of a lesser sentence than the witness would otherwise be exposed to. Such plea bargaining, as it is called, has been approved as lawful and proper and is expressly provided for in the rules of this court. However, a witness who hopes to gain more favorable treatment may have a reason to make a false statement because the witness wants to strike a good bargain with the Government. So while a witness of that kind may be entirely truthful when testifying, you should consider such testimony with more caution than the testimony of other witnesses.

If Defendant Doesn't Testify

A defendant has a right not to testify. The fact that Andre Clark did not take the witness stand cannot be considered by you for any purpose, and no adverse inference whatsoever can be drawn against the defendant by reason of his decision not to take the stand.

If Defendant Does Testify

A defendant has a right not to testify. If a defendant does testify, however, that testimony should be weighed and considered, and the defendant's credibility determined, in the same way as that of any other witness.

The defendant is charged with a violation of Title 18, United States Code, Sections 2113(a) and (d) and Section 2. Title 18, United States Code, Sections 2113 (a) and (d), make it a Federal crime for anyone to take from a person or presence of someone else by force and violence or by intimidation any property or money in the possession of a federally insured bank, and in the process of so doing to assault any person or put in jeopardy the life of any person by the use of a dangerous weapon or device.

The defendant can be found guilty of this offense only if all of the following facts are proved beyond a reasonable doubt:

> First: That the defendant knowingly took from the person or the presence of the person described in the indictment money or property then in the possession of a federally insured bank, as charged;
>
> Second: That the defendant did so by means of force or violence or by means of intimidation;
>
> Third: That the defendant assaulted or put in jeopardy the life of some person by the use of a dangerous weapon or device while engaged in taking the property or money, as charged.

A "federally insured bank" means any bank the deposits of which are insured by the Federal Deposit Insurance Corporation. There has been a stipulation, or agreement, between the parties that the Nita City branch of the Main Street Bank was a federally insured bank.

To take "by means of intimidation" is to say or do something in such a way that a person of ordinary sensibilities would be fearful of bodily harm; it is not necessary to prove that the alleged victim was actually frightened, and neither is it necessary to show that the behavior of the defendant was so violent that it was likely to cause terror, panic, or hysteria.

A "dangerous weapon or device" includes anything capable of being readily operated or wielded by one person to inflict severe bodily harm or injury on another person.

To "put in jeopardy the life of any person by the use of a dangerous weapon or device" means, then, to expose someone else to a risk of death by the use of such a dangerous weapon or device.

Aiding and Abetting

The indictment charges the defendant with the substantive count discussed above and also with violating Title 18, United States Code, Section 2. This section provides as follows:

> Whoever commits an offense against the United States or aids, abets, counsels, commands, induces or procures its commission, is punishable as a principal. In addition, whoever willfully causes an act to be done which if directly performed by him or another would be an offense against the United States, is punishable as a principal.

Thus, the guilt of a defendant in a criminal case may be proved without evidence that the defendant personally did every act involved in the commission of the crime charged. The law recognizes that ordinarily, anything a person can do for one's self may also be accomplished through direction of another person as an agent or by acting together with, or under the direction of, another person or persons in a joint effort.

So if the acts or conduct of an agent, employee, or other associate of the defendant are willfully directed or authorized by the defendant or if the defendant aided and abetted another person by willfully joining together with that person in the commission of a crime, then the law holds the defendant responsible for the conduct of that other person just as though the defendant had personally engaged in such conduct.

However, before any defendant can be held criminally responsible for the conduct of others, it is necessary that the defendant willfully associate in some way with the crime and willfully participate in it. Mere presence at the scene of a crime and even knowledge that a crime is being committed are not sufficient to establish that a defendant either directed or aided and abetted the crime. You must find beyond a reasonable doubt that the defendant was a willful participant and not merely a knowing spectator.

The question of punishment should never be considered by the jury in any way in deciding the case. If a defendant is convicted the matter of punishment is for the judge to determine later.

Any verdict you reach in the jury room, whether guilty or not guilty, must represent the considered judgment of each juror.

In order to return a verdict, it is necessary that each juror agree thereto. In other words, your verdict must be unanimous.

(Explain verdict form)

IN THE UNITED STATES DISTRICT COURT

FOR THE NORTHERN DISTRICT OF NITA

UNITED STATES OF AMERICA)
)
v.) JURY VERDICT
)
ANDRE CLARK)

We, the jury, return the following verdict and each of us concurs in this verdict:

(Choose the appropriate verdict)

1. We, the jury, find the Defendant, Andre Clark, guilty of the offense of Bank Robbery.

   _____
   Foreperson

2. We, the jury, find the Defendant, Andre Clark, not guilty.

   _____
   Foreperson